D0358922

MEDIA & CENSORSHIP

Roger Thomas

Heinemann
LIBRARY

www.heinemann.co.uk/library
Visit our website to find out more information about **Heinemann Library** books.

To order:
☎ Phone 44 (0) 1865 888066
▤ Send a fax to 44 (0) 1865 314091
▢ Visit the Heinemann Bookshop at www.heinemann.co.uk/library to browse our catalogue and order online.

First published in Great Britain by Heinemann Library, Halley Court, Jordan Hill, Oxford OX2 8EJ, a division of Reed Educational and Professional Publishing Ltd. Heinemann is a registered trademark of Reed Educational & Professional Publishing Limited.

OXFORD MELBOURNE AUCKLAND JOHANNESBURG BLANTYRE
GABORONE IBADAN PORTSMOUTH NH (USA) CHICAGO

Designed by Tinstar Design (www.tinstar.co.uk)
Originated by Ambassador Litho Ltd
Printed in Hong Kong/China

ISBN 0 431 03554 7

05 04 03 02 01
10 9 8 7 6 5 4 3 2 1

British Library Cataloguing in Publication Data
Thomas, Roger
    Media and censorship. – (What's at issue?)
    1. Media and censorship – Great Britain – Juvenile literature
    2. Pluralism (Social sciences) – Great Britain – Juvenile literature
    I. Title
    306

Acknowledgements
The Publishers would like to thank the following for permission to reproduce photographs:
AKG Photo: Marion Kalter p34; British Board of Film Classification: p24; Corbis: pp8, 9, Hulton-Deutsch p13, John Garrett p21, AFP p22, Matthew Mendelsohn p41; Cumulus: p33, Trevor Clifford p16; Hulton Getty: pp38, 39; Kobal Collection: pp11, 23, 26, 27, 42, 43; Mirrorpix: p15; Radio Times: p6; Rex Features: p14, Edward Webb p25, Sipa Press pp28, 31, 32; Stone: p30; Tudor Photography: pp5, 7, 18, 19, 29, 36

Cover photograph: Pictor.

Our thanks to Julie Turner (School Counsellor, Banbury School, Oxfordshire) for her comments in the preparation of this book.

Any words appearing in the text in bold, **like this**, are explained in the Glossary.

Contents

Introduction

Censorship means changing or controlling the information we get from the media. It can happen to all kinds of media, including books, newspapers, magazines, television, radio, film, video, computer software and the Internet. It can happen to all kinds of artforms, too, including literature, the theatre and even music. It can happen for both good and bad reasons – perhaps to prevent young children from seeing things that will frighten them, or perhaps to prevent people from spreading information that might help to overthrow an **oppressive** government. It can be carried out by many different people, ranging from government departments to the business people who own media companies. This book describes some of the different ways in which censorship has been carried out in the past and how it happens today.

What censorship is

One dictionary definition of a censor is 'an official with the authority to examine letters, books, periodicals, plays, films etc and to cut out anything regarded as immoral or, in time of war, helpful to the enemy', with censorship being 'the function or duties of a censor'.

For as long as human communication has existed, there have been times and places when one group of people has wanted to withhold information from another group of people, or to control how information is presented, or actually to change or falsify information that is available. This book will describe some of the ways this has been done in the past and how it is being done today.

However, we need to bear in mind exactly what censorship is. Strictly speaking, to censor something means to alter or take away information from something, or to change the way in which information is presented. Censorship can be imposed on any kind of information, including books, newspapers, magazines, radio and TV broadcasts, websites, advertising and even art and music.

Who does the censoring, and why?

Throughout history, different types of authority have been in charge of censorship, for different reasons. In our society today, censorship is governed by laws and by the guidelines laid down by various organizations that deal with the many different media to which we have access. Some of these organizations are referred to elsewhere in this book.

However, censorship can also come about as a result of religious or political beliefs, or **taboos**, or even for economic reasons. Different ideas about what should be censored (and what is deemed to be acceptable) exist in different cultures in the world today. Within any individual culture ideas about what should be censored are constantly changing, although such changes may take one or more generations to become apparent.

Where censorship begins and ends

This is a very important aspect of the whole subject of censorship. For example, if a video is banned from the shops completely, can it be said to have been censored? A good example is a film by Abel Ferrera, *The Driller Killer*, about a serial killer who murders his victims with an electric drill. This was banned from video release for a period of fifteen years after it appeared in the cinema because of the excessive violence in the film. The video was not even available in a censored version. When it finally did become available on video, it was because improvements in **special effects** in new films made the violence in this older film seem unbelievable to cinema audiences. It was unlikely that anyone would be inspired to attempt copy-cat crimes after seeing it. This example contrasts with that of *Flesh Gordon*, a sex comedy parody of the classic science fiction film *Flash Gordon*. This was released on video with some of the sex scenes cut, so could truly be said to have been censored. So is the banning of something the equivalent of censoring its entire content? What if the ban is subsequently lifted?

Before and after

To complicate matters further, censorship can be applied either before or after a book, film, recording or whatever is made available to the public. *The Little Red Schoolbook*, first published in Denmark in 1969, was a book of advice to school pupils based on **left-wing political principles** and with a section devoted to teenage sexuality. When the book was published in the UK in 1971, the British courts declared the book to be obscene (the legal definition being that the material in question may 'deprave and corrupt' those who read it) and demanded that the book be republished with changes made to this section. This meant that there were both censored and uncensored versions of the book.

Such issues as this – exactly what constitutes censorship and how cultural changes can affect the kind of material that may be censored – are themes that constantly recur when we look at this subject.

This book was censored when it was published in the UK.

5

What censorship is not

Having thought about what censorship is, it is equally important to think about other ways in which information is restricted, but which do not amount to censorship. The issue is often unclear.

Personal liberty and freedom of information

Here are just a few ways in which information is changed or withheld from us in our daily lives. Can you decide if any of these examples are forms of censorship?

- Medical information being withheld from the family of a dying patient
- Song lyrics that contain **expletives** being changed in a version for radio use
- Someone who is unwilling to tell you how much they earn
- The fact that girls who model clothes are usually very thin.

Each of these situations is an example of information being restricted or controlled. It could be argued that the patient's family have a right to know all the details of their loved one's health. On the other hand, if the family does not have the necessary knowledge to fully understand the situation but simply knows that the patient is dying, might a lot of possibly incomprehensible details just add to their grief? The song lyrics may simply be changed because the record company thinks that the recorded version will sell for reasons of notoriety, while the altered version ensures that the song also gets radio play. Many people do not like to talk about their income to people they otherwise know very well, yet if, say, they borrow some money from a bank, they will probably be obliged to state their salary. The fashion industry is often accused of persuading young women that it is important to be thin, thus bringing about eating disorders such as anorexia nervosa. Yet one famous fashion designer has said that the only reason the industry uses thin models is because it is easier to make clothes look good on them (he compared them to coat-hangers!).

These examples show that there are many ways in which information and ideas can be controlled or changed, which are not really the same as censorship as defined on pages 4–5. This is especially true in modern society where information and ideas are conveyed so easily in so many different ways.

This is a film review, which appeared in the listings magazine *Radio Times*. By describing scenes in the film, which may be unacceptable to some viewers, it shows how information can be controlled without it actually being removed or altered.

CB4 ★★★
12.20am–1.45am BBC2
Sun 00.20–01.45
More like *Fear of a Black Hat* than *This Is Spinal Tap*, this comedy was co-written by its star, *Saturday Night Live* alumnus Chris Rock. Although it occasionally lacks cohesion, the film takes several well-aimed pot shots at both gangsta rap and the culture that engendered it. Surprisingly, considering it was directed by a woman, Tamra Davis, it somewhat ducks the issue of sexism, and many will find Khandi Alexander's character hard to take. But Rock and his rappers clearly have a ball, and Eddie Murphy's brother, Charlie, appears as the convict who inspires the band's name (CB4 stands for Cell Block 4) and image. Contains swearing, sex scenes, drug abuse and nudity. *DP*
(US 1993, 18, 85 min) (S) *1368172*

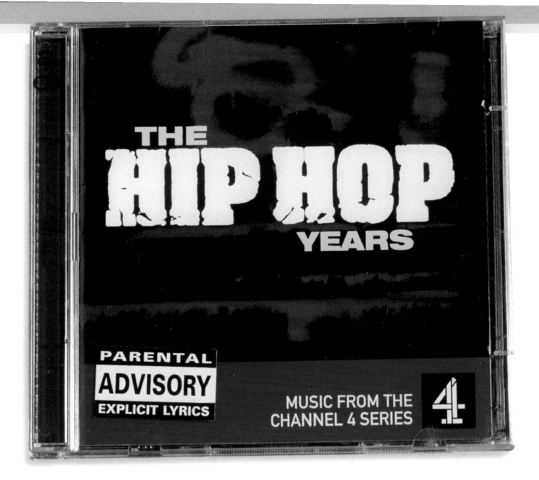

CDs very often have stickers on the cover if the song lyrics contain expletives.

Responsibility and awareness

There are many situations where we as individuals find ourselves responsible for controlling information. Here are some examples:

- A child wanting to stay up late to watch a horror film on TV
- Shouting at someone to prevent them expressing their point of view
- Keeping a diary which no one else knows about.

In the first example, we may wish to make sure the child goes to bed instead, because the film will be too frightening or may affect the child's behaviour. In the second example to 'shout someone down' is to control information in an aggressive and repressive way – but what if the person being shouted down is saying something very offensive? You may

find it important to keep a private diary, and there is no reason why you should not. If something happens to you, however, there may be clues in your diary that will help others to help you – so perhaps you should at least let your best friend or an adult you can trust know that you keep this diary and where you hide it.

ALL KINDS OF CONTROLS

As we have seen, there are many different ways in which information can be withheld or controlled. Some may be desirable and others undesirable, but many are desirable in some situations but not in others. Working out which is which is often very difficult.

The origins of censorship

We cannot know whether prehistoric societies practised any form of censorship. It is possible, for example, that cave artists were discouraged by their culture from recording too many unsuccessful hunts! But it is more likely that true censorship first emerged when human society became more organized and sophisticated and the power of information to affect society was first recognized.

Ancient civilizations

During the period when Greek and Roman culture dominated Europe, learning was not formally divided into science, art, literature and so on. For example, the Roman poet Lucretius wrote a book which attempted to explain scientific phenomena in the form of poetry. Ideas about what information people should be allowed to know and what areas of thinking should be discouraged were often strongly connected with **moral philosophy** and religion.

As there were no mass media, information was mainly passed on through teaching and learned debate. The Greek philosopher Socrates (c.470–399 BC) was one of the first thinkers to be a victim of state censorship. Socrates believed that free discussion on any subject was central to the quality of life – his was the first formal philosophy of **intellectual freedom**. The governing body of the Greek capital, the Athenian Assembly, wanted to censor the teachings of Socrates so that they would support the religious and moral thinking of the day.

Socrates refused to allow this. He was charged with **heresy** and corrupting his students, and was sentenced to death.

Interestingly, one of Socrates' most important pupils, the philosopher Plato (c.428–c.348 BC) took the opposite view. For example, Plato thought that any art, literature or music which could not be used actively to teach good moral principles – acceptable behaviour and an understanding of good and evil – should actually be banned. This even extended to preventing parents or carers telling children stories that did not follow these rules. Plato outlined these ideas in his book *The Republic*.

Plato outlined his ideas for a formal system of censorship in his book *The Republic*.

8

In Ancient Rome, **freedom of speech** was regarded as a privilege granted only to those in authority. The poets Ovid and Juvenal were both banished for being too outspoken, the emperor Caligula had a dissenting writer burned alive, while the emperor Nero banished his critics and had their books burned. On the other hand, while there was political **oppression**, Roman attitudes to sexuality were much more relaxed compared to today. For example, highly **explicit** pictures advertising a brothel were found by archaeologists on the walls of the Roman city of Pompeii. This is a good example of how the kind of information that is censored changes over time and across different cultures.

Early censorship in Britain and Europe

When Christianity became the main religion of the Roman Empire, censorship became closely associated with the preservation of orthodox Christian beliefs. For example, in AD 496 Pope Gelasius issued a list of forbidden books that conflicted with the established ideas of Christianity. The **Inquisition**, set up by Pope Gregory IX in 1231, was responsible for religious censorship as well as burning supposed witches. After Protestantism displaced Roman Catholicism as the official religion of Great Britain in 1534, King Henry VIII insisted that all book manuscripts were submitted to the church for approval before publication. This lasted until 1695.

Since this time, many laws and declarations have aimed to eliminate oppression and censorship of this kind.

King Henry VIII enforced religious censorship to ensure no books on Catholicism were published.

9

The mass media

We have seen some early examples of censorship, but it has really only been since the beginnings of the mass media that censorship has become the very complex issue it is today.

The power of print

Even when compared to the Internet, the printed word remains one of the most effective ways of circulating information. Printed material is completely self-contained – you do not need a computer, TV or radio or anything else. At the most basic level all that is required is a flat surface and the means to make a mark upon it. For example, during the Second World War, the French Resistance would deface posters put up by the occupying **Nazi** forces. Even this simple act helped to encourage the French people to stand up to their conquerors, by using the Nazis' own posters against them.

> ## *FACT*
>
> ● *Before mass literacy, information was normally spread by word of mouth. Educated people wrote letters and manuscripts but, as many people could not read, much information was delivered to the masses by town criers or by officials who read out laws and proclamations. The invention of the printing press made it possible to produce any number of copies relatively quickly and cheaply, and as literacy became more widespread it became possible to circulate information in a permanent form.*

It is also relatively easy to print, duplicate or photocopy information. This has both good and bad implications. On the one hand, it enables, say, the victims of political **oppression** to encourage others to fight back by producing **underground** publications. An example is the **'samizdat'** publications that circulated in the **Soviet Union**, produced on cheap manual duplicators and containing material that was unacceptable to the regime. On the other hand, it is equally easy to print and distribute racist or other offensive material. But should this be censored? Or should people be allowed to express any views?

Today there are various controls in place which affect what kinds of printed material can be made available to the public. In the UK there are existing Acts of Parliament, such as the Obscene Publications Act that controls sexually oriented material. There are also organizations such as the Press Council, which polices the editorial content of magazines and newspapers. Other countries have government bodies, such as the Office of Film and Literature **Classification** (OFLC) in Australia, which deal with censorship. As with all aspects of censorship in a democratic country, their activities are sometimes controversial. For example, some celebrities have complained to the Press Council that newspaper reports about their personal lives have been intrusive. The counter-argument is that celebrities are successful precisely because they sell themselves to the public. The public are therefore entitled to know how they conduct their lives because, for instance through buying a pop star's records or by funding the monarchy via taxation, the public is paying for their lifestyles. What do you think?

Broadcasting

Because the technology of broadcasting is much more complex than that of print, there are more ways of censoring the medium. Many supposedly 'live' broadcasts can be manipulated in various ways. Live TV shows can have a recorded alternative ready to roll if something goes wrong, or be broadcast with a delay of a few seconds to allow 'emergency' censorship. Interviewees who use **expletives** may find a 'beep' recorded over each of the offending words, although this can often be dependent on the time of transmission. For example, in the UK, TV programmes broadcast after 9.00 pm are deemed to be suitable for adults. This can produce some **paradoxical** results. The gangster film *Pulp Fiction* has been broadcast complete with the many expletives in the dialogue, yet no film critic discussing the film on TV even after the 9.00 pm **watershed** would use the same kind of language in describing the film. Is this censorship? If not, why not? Why is one acceptable and not the other?

Recorded media and the Internet

Audio and video recordings are also easy to produce and distribute, with all manner of material being available, legally or not. The Internet is global in scope and costs next to nothing to use, relying largely on **filtering** software produced by the service providers.

Given such a diverse **media landscape**, the whole question of censorship is extremely complex.

Pulp Fiction is a film that can only be shown after the watershed because of the number of expletives it contains.

Books

For many centuries in Western society the book was the only means of preserving the written word with any certainty. Although today it is possible to buy inexpensive books on most subjects, originally all books were written individually by hand, usually by monks. This meant, of course, that they were relatively rare and certainly expensive, and for, say, a medieval scholar to possess even half a dozen books written by others meant that he was both very wise and very wealthy.

This association between books and scholarship persists today. There remains a certain mystique about buying, reading and owning books, particularly as there are now so many other ways in which information can be stored and passed on. Also, because the British class structure has its origins in the medieval divide between nobles and peasants, books remain associated with society's educated elite. Even though books today are entirely commonplace, you will still hear talk of people whose abilities are said to be inadequate because they are based on 'book learning' rather than experience, and the phrase 'So-and-so always has his/her nose in a book' is still used disparagingly. This happens to be one of the themes of the Disney animated film *Beauty and the Beast*, which offers a demonstration of this kind of thinking – perhaps ironically, as no doubt many of the film's audience will never have read the story in a book.

The other important feature that is still associated with books is the skill of literacy. This is again associated with the ruling elite and again now commonplace (although by no means universal). These factors were, however, to have interesting implications for the first example below.

Some controversial books

The censorship of books has often centred both on the language used in them and on their content. One of the most famous examples of this is D H Lawrence's novel *Lady Chatterley's Lover*, a tale of the relationship between an aristocratic Englishwoman and her gamekeeper. Despite their very different backgrounds they are united by a love of life, which is described explicitly in terms of their sexual encounters and through their use of the kind of **colloquial** sexual language many people routinely use during such intimate moments. However, despite its ordinariness in the real world, to place such material between the covers of a book was regarded as obscene. As a result, despite having been written in the early part of the 20th century, *Lady Chatterley's Lover* remained unpublished until 1960, a full 30 years after Lawrence's death. The publishers, Penguin Books, were promptly prosecuted and the ensuing court case became one of the most celebrated causes in the history of literary censorship. It soon emerged that many of those involved were not so much concerned about the content of the book than about what kind of person might read it. This had little to do with the more sophisticated idea of people being inspired to carry out particular actions by what they read, but rather more to do with the ancient mystique about literacy and social class described above. One person present at the trial said he would not have wanted his gamekeeper to read the book! In the event, the book stayed in print, as it is to this day.

Another example shows how some authors are happy to respond to censorship in their own way. In the sixties the American author Gore Vidal wrote a novel called *Myra Breckinridge*, a sharp-witted piece of social **satire** in which the leading character, Myra, is a **transsexual**. Despite being very well reviewed by many leading publications such as the *New York Times* and the *New Statesman*, the book was associated with pornography because of its use of **expletive** words for various bodily parts. When Vidal wrote a sequel, *Myron* (Myra having had her sex-change operation reversed), he mockingly substituted the surnames of various officials and anti-pornography campaigners for the words in question. *Myron* therefore contains numerous references to 'Powells' and 'Father Hills', and even the odd 'Whizzer White' – but no expletives.

D H Lawrence: not recommended reading for gamekeepers.

Newspapers

This has always been a very controversial area, especially in the UK which traditionally supports the idea of a **free press**. This contrasts with, for example, the former **Soviet Union**, where the main national newspaper, *Pravda*, was under the control of the government and supported its aims. There are many conflicting demands on newspapers. On the one hand, they are expected to be independent of any outside influence, as it is supposedly their job to objectively inform the population of important events at home and abroad. On the other hand, readers also expect newspapers to express opinions yet tend to buy those that reinforce their own prejudices.

The language of journalism

Even the language of reporting is shot through with prejudice. A good example is the use of the noun 'youth'. The

TRY THIS

The philosopher and critic Walter Benjamin has pointed out that there is in fact no such thing as **objective** news reporting. Instead, every item of news is always mixed with the prejudiced opinion of whoever is doing the reporting. This is easy to prove by simply taking any newspaper story and re-writing it from the different points of view of the various parties involved. Try it – it's surprisingly easy. You could also buy a selection of newspapers on one day and compare the way the same story is interpreted in each newspaper.

dictionary defines the word as simply meaning 'a young man', yet it is mostly used in connection with young men whose behaviour is held to be undesirable or suspect. 'A group of youths' may be reported as having stolen a car. But you will not read about 'a group of youths' queuing quietly for tickets to a concert of classical music, even if there is a group of them and they are indeed young men. While the word 'youths' is not in itself prejudicial, it is to the advantage of newspapers and other news media to use it

Violence is routinely depicted in the press without comment.

in this way. It appears to carry no opinion, yet everyone knows that in this context it should be taken to mean something like 'dodgy-looking young blokes who are either committing a crime or who look as though they might'.

Who censors newspapers?

The 'youth' example is not really censorship – nothing is actually removed from the newspaper – but a more subtle form of information control. However, there are various people and organizations who do find it in their interests to try to censor newspapers. One common example is that of **media barons**, who own one or more newspapers but who also have other business interests, which may involve other media or other enterprises altogether. For example, if a newspaper proprietor is attempting to do business with a country that has a bad human rights record, he may attempt to restrict or influence the reporting in his newspaper of events in that country. Restrictions can be imposed on newspaper reporting if certain material is deemed to be undesirable. Often this is beneficial – for example, a **minor** accused of a crime may have his/her name withheld while the case is proceeding. But these powers can also be controversial if they allow the government to conceal activities which affect the public interest.

DOUBLE STANDARDS? OR SELF-CENSORSHIP?

Newspapers offer a 'snapshot' of the conventions that govern society. The images on these pages are an interesting example. One depicts an act of violence that would surely be condemned and reviled by ordinary people in different societies throughout the world. The other clearly implies sex, which is a normal part of adult life. Yet the first image is generally acceptable, while the second can still provoke objections from many people. Newspapers offer interesting insights into how cultures create their own standards as to what ideas and images should be available to the public.

On the other hand, sexual imagery in newspaper photography can still raise objections.

Magazines

Magazines are relatively easy to produce and distribute, which means that they can be used very effectively as vehicles for contentious material and can also be very adaptable when they encounter censorship. In politically oppressed countries, **underground** magazines can be produced on inexpensive copying equipment and distributed without having to use official channels, making them hard to censor. The **satirical** magazine *Krokodil*, published in Russia, was a thorn in the side of the Soviet regime for many years.

In the UK, the situation is less crucial, and the main areas of magazine censorship relate to sexual imagery and language. Many of the potential problems surrounding adult glamour and sex magazines are simply solved by placing them out of reach of children – hence the term 'top-shelf' magazines. Some newsagents also place them in opaque bags or fasten them closed with sticky tape.

The bag around this 'lads' mag' enables it to carry an assortment of free gifts while also conveniently censoring the cover.

MAGAZINES, THE LAW AND MORALITY

The censorship of magazines in the UK is largely covered by the Obscene Publications Act, but complaints can also be referred to the Press Council and the Advertising Standards Authority. The moral aspects of magazine censorship are often questioned by people who are in favour of censorship reform. They point out, for example, that magazines devoted to firearms are freely available, which may encourage gun-related violence. Magazines depicting sex and/or nudity, however, are subject to far stricter controls despite the fact that both are not only relatively harmless in themselves but are in fact very ordinary aspects of normal living.

This may well be partly to stop children having access to them but it also has the effect of preventing browsing, as readers are prevented from inspecting the contents of the magazine on the shelf.

New Worlds

A rather more interesting historical case involved the science fiction magazine *New Worlds*, which serialized an anti-racist novel by the American author Norman Spinrad in the late 1960s. The narrative made use of various **colloquial expletives**. These, while not subject to censorship prior to publication, caused a storm of protest among members of the mainstream literary and political establishments. One of the main reasons for this was that, as the magazine was generally held to have artistic value, it received government funding in the form of a grant from the Arts Council of Great Britain. This led to the rather simplistic conclusion that taxpayers' money was being used to subsidize 'filth', with the result that questions were asked in Parliament as to why this should be allowed.

While issues of this kind were not unusual, it is interesting to note that D H Lawrence's novel *Lady Chatterley's Lover* (see pages 12–13) had survived a similar period of controversy in the same decade. *New Worlds*, however, was an independently published magazine without the financial backing of a company like Penguin Books, which had published Lawrence's novel. Any difficulties of this kind, therefore, could prove disastrous – and they did. The newsagents W H Smith decided to stop selling the magazine because of the debate surrounding it. This was a very serious blow, as this nationwide chain of shops was (and remains) crucial to the UK circulation of any magazine. When the publisher of *New Worlds* visited the W H Smith management to try to persuade them to continue stocking the magazine, he cited the example of *Mayfair*, a top-shelf glamour magazine which the chain routinely stocked. He argued that *New Worlds* could hardly be more controversial than a magazine full of sex stories and pictures of naked women. The publisher was told that *Mayfair* was a completely different case – unlike the specialist *New Worlds*, *Mayfair* sold many thousands of copies throughout the country! Do you think W H Smith was genuinely concerned about the content of *New Worlds* magazine, or were they simply looking for an excuse to stop selling a magazine which didn't sell very many copies? Does this example show how the power to control information can be used for economic reasons?

Comics

In the UK the censorship of comics has rarely been a serious issue. Their history as a form of entertainment for children – paid for, and therefore screened by, adults – has ensured that they have rarely attracted censorship. There was however, a campaign against horror comics, and there have been occasional objections to violence, such as in the case of *2000 AD*, or instances when adult comics such as *Viz* have been placed where children can pick them up.

In other countries, however, the situation is more complex. In the USA and Japan, for example, there is a long tradition of comics that are specifically produced for adult readers. The contents of these comics often reflect this in their handling of human relationships, and will often include sex and sexuality and more realistic forms of violence, such as domestic abuse. For the most part, these elements are simply included in the general narrative among other themes designed to appeal to adults.

Side-stepping the censor?

One good example of the form is the series of stories, written during the 1980s by Reed Waller and his partner Kate Worley, about a dancer named Omaha. Omaha, like all the other characters in the stories, is in fact an animal – in her case, a cat. However, the illustrations are heavily **anthropomorphic**, depicting the 'animals' as looking very much like human beings. This is a standard technique used in animal stories for children, such as *Rupert the Bear*.

However, the writers of *Omaha, the Cat Dancer* make it clear that the stories are really about adult human beings, in exactly the way that the Rupert stories are really about children. The stories deal with a variety of subjects significant to adults – sex and relationships, moral dilemmas, family problems, abuse in the workplace, corporate greed and so on – but present these in a highly **explicit** way.

The American cartoon stories featuring *Omaha* raise many issues relating to comics and censorship.

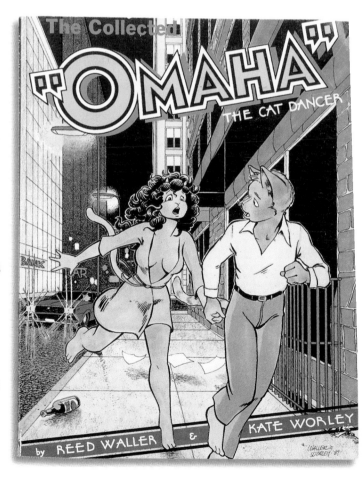

The writers claimed that they had been looking for a way to handle these subjects in a cartoon format, but that cartoon human beings simply looked 'wrong', whereas the traditional 'furry animal' type of cartoon character simply looked 'right'. Many of the sex scenes in the *Omaha* stories would be regarded as extremely pornographic if they had people in them. But is it strictly possible to produce pornography without using human beings? (One humorous website has addressed this very issue by producing 'pornography' featuring garden furniture instead of people!) Or might this just be a way of avoiding the censorship of what would otherwise be unacceptable material? When does an animal cartoon become pornography? In the UK, *Omaha* was simply sold in shops specializing in adult comics, along with hundreds of other titles. What do you think?

THE COMICS CODE

The best-known example of the content of comics being subject to control is the US Comics Code. By the mid-1950s American comics had become a sophisticated medium. However, many writers and illustrators were using them to convey narratives and images which would have been restricted or banned altogether had they appeared in a more mainstream medium such as the cinema. These were mainly scenes involving exceptionally gory or horrific events. Most of the comics involved, such as *Weird Tales* published by the EC company, featured horror or science fiction stories. Parents became concerned about this and in 1955 the Comics Code was set up, which placed restrictions on the presentation of explicitly violent and horrific material. Many comics were obliged to close down as a result of this. However, with the subsequent rise of comics as an adult artform, many publishers now produce titles without Code approval for sale through specialist dealers rather than through news-stands where children might see them – a simple solution that satisfies all involved.

Radio

The censorship of radio broadcasting is so routine as to be built into the very process of making radio programmes and it relates to both **talk radio** and music. Ironically, because it is so widespread and used so efficiently, many people are unaware of it. This is typical of the most successful instances of censorship – not only is information withheld from recipients, but the fact that this information is being withheld is itself successfully withheld. This is a perfect example of the ultimate **paradox** affecting the anti-censorship **lobby**. Those who wish to eliminate censorship altogether can never succeed, simply because, by definition, they will never know about it when it is used most effectively.

Pulling the plug

Live talk radio broadcasts are often censored in quite sophisticated ways. For example, when a listener calls a phone-in show, he or she is answered by a researcher who asks the caller to state their question or point of view. The researcher then decides if the subject is suitable, and whether the caller appears to be sincere and unlikely to be disruptive on air. If the researcher is not satisfied, the caller may be given a reason why their call will not be included. This may be genuine or not, and can range from 'We've already got someone waiting on the line with a similar question' to 'We've got a lot of callers just now, so we'll try to fit you in, but please feel free to hang up at any time if you can't wait.' In fact, of course, the call is quietly 'forgotten'.

If the caller does succeed in reaching the radio host or their guest, their call may be cut short if they appear to be speaking inappropriately on air, such as subjecting the host or a studio guest to verbal abuse, or swearing.

TRY THIS:

Censorship-spotting: a fun game for radio listeners!

Skilled radio presenters will know how to cut off a controversial phone-in caller while making it look as if their contribution has finished. The conversation may go something like this:

CALLER: ...and I think the whole issue of the Millennium Dome is a complete scandal – all that money wasted...

PRESENTER: Yes...

CALLER: ...I think all the politicians and businessmen involved should be executed and have their heads hung up over the ticket barriers...

PRESENTER (making light of the situation, while the caller is cut off, although they may not realize this): Ha ha! You mean like they used to do at the Tower of London! Well, this just goes to show how strong the feelings are about this project. Thanks for your call – now let's hear from Mandy who's calling from Droitwich...

The caller, of course, may by this point be claiming that the Prime Minister is an alien and that the whole problem is the fault of unmarried mothers, all of whom should be put to death – and so on!

Try listening to as many phone-in **slots** as you can for a week or two to see if you can spot any censorship of this kind.

Paul McCartney's music is enjoyed by several generations of listeners, but his lyrics have also attracted a form of censorship.

Controversial music

Because radio is such an accessible medium – there is no licence fee, and radios are cheap enough for children to own – this sensitivity is perhaps understandable. However, even pop music can cause problems. BBC Radio, for example, has been known to ban songs which have lyrics which deal with sex, drugs and politics. These have included 'Relax' by Frankie Goes to Hollywood, which contained some possible references to gay sex; 'God Save the Queen', by the Sex Pistols, which supposedly called the Queen a 'moron' (it didn't) and Paul McCartney's 'Give Ireland Back to the Irish', which protested against the British military presence in Northern Ireland. Some bands, such as The Beautiful South, have recorded special versions of songs for radio use because the originals contained **expletives**, in a commercially-motivated form of self-censorship. Is this reasonable and sensible? In this case, the expletives were used in describing an unsatisfactory relationship in a realistic and very articulate style. Might this have devalued the original idea behind the song? What do you think?

Television

Television is without doubt the most intrusive medium of all. It is present in most households, where adults will often not be aware of what is being watched by children, but at the same time it is an important source of information and entertainment.

What gets censored, how and why?

Some examples are:

- News reports can be censored, such as during the recent period when the voices of people associated with the **IRA** were not allowed to be heard directly on television for fear that this would somehow imply that television offered a sympathetic **platform** for the promotion of terrorism. The idea backfired completely, as newsreaders would constantly refer to the restrictions and the words of, for example, the **Sinn Fein** leader Gerry Adams would be re-recorded by an actor, usually using a bad Irish accent! The result was as bizarre as it sounds and succeeded only in drawing attention to how television can be subjected to particularly crass forms of censorship.

- Films on television can be censored or subjected to other forms of control. Films will often be cut slightly to fit into an available **slot** in the schedules. When this happens, it is highly likely that any cuts made will be of scenes involving violence or sex – although this may not be

The voice of Gerry Adams, leader of Sinn Fein, has been subject to an odd form of censorship during television broadcasts.

indicated by the broadcasting company. On other occasions, films will be deliberately edited for these reasons. This will be acknowledged in such places as the review columns of the broadcasting listings magazine, *Radio Times*. Also, care is generally taken to ensure that films with adult content are broadcast after the 9.00 pm **watershed**, with particularly adult-oriented material being shown very late at night.

● Other measures have also been tried, with varying degrees of success. One memorable example is the Channel 4 warning triangle. Channel 4 sometimes broadcasts sophisticated, intellectually demanding **arthouse** films, which can include sexual activity and other potentially controversial material. However, this material is not necessarily the main theme of an **art film**, but is usually just one element in it, and the film's title will rarely allude to it. While a simple sex comedy like *Confessions of a Window Cleaner* has a title which implies a degree of lewdness, there is no reason to anticipate from the title or a plot summary (a group of women contrive the deaths of their husbands) that an arthouse film such as Peter Greenaway's *Drowning by Numbers* contains far more sexual material. For this reason, Channel 4 adopted a system of adding a small triangular mark to one corner of the screen whenever such a film was being broadcast. In the event, this system simply allowed viewers who were hoping deliberately to track down such material to do so with greater ease – not at all the audience Channel 4 had in mind. The idea was quietly dropped.

● TV advertisements tend not to be censored as such, but are more likely to be withdrawn altogether if any controversial material attracts complaints. There are various bodies, such as the

Some arthouse films contain material that is not suitable for younger viewers. TV companies may censor the film as a result.

Advertising Standards Authority, which monitor this. Advertisements for certain products, such as cigarettes, are in any event not permitted on television at all. However, there are some instances when the traditional restrictions faced by UK television advertising can produce some unfortunate results. The government's first AIDS awareness effort was tastefully removed from its subject matter, to the extent that in a television advertising campaign the disease was represented by an earthquake! This contrasts with an anti-AIDS campaign on Swedish television, which showed a young woman playfully twanging a condom against her lover's bottom, pointing out to him their importance in preventing the spread of AIDS. Which do you think probably worked best?

Film

The relationship between the cinema and the censor has always been a fraught and complex one, but its earliest origins lie elsewhere, in pictorial art. As you can see by looking in an art book or gallery, both classical and modern art often include images of violence and nudity. These elements were frequently a part of the subject matter of classical painting, which often drew on history, with paintings of gory battles, and myth, with the idea that gods, goddesses and other mythical beings would not need to wear clothes often being used as an excuse to depict nudity.

How films are censored

With the rise in popularity of the cinema, the **British Board of Film Classification (BBFC)** was created in order to monitor the content of films. Other countries have similar bodies, such as the Office of Film and Literature **Classification** in Australia. One major concern was that children should not be allowed to watch unsuitable material. This led to the creation of a certification system that indicated which audiences a given film was intended for. More importantly, it allowed cinema staff to prevent children from entering a cinema to see a film if its certificate did not permit this. Originally, there were only three types of certificate.

The BBFC monitors the content of films and decides what certificate each film is given.

'IF IT MOVES, IT'S RUDE'

The idea that immobile images were 'art' and therefore acceptable fed into popular culture. The result was that early **erotic** theatre **revues** of the late 19th and early 20th centuries, such as those performed at the famous Windmill Theatre in London, relied heavily on **tableaux vivants**. These revues would generally begin with the curtain closed. A singer stood in front of it, singing a short narrative song with some historical or mythical theme – say, a story about the goddess Venus. The curtain would then open to reveal a group of more-or-less nude women standing stock-still, with poses and scenery that depicted this mythological world. This was considered acceptable for adult audiences due to its resemblance to classical art, giving rise to the Windmill's motto, 'If it moves, it's rude'. However, when the cinema became popular, it became clear that this medium's ability to realistically show all manner of things moving about would attract censorship.

A 'U' (standing for 'universal') certificate meant that anyone, child or adult, could see the film. An 'A' ('adult') certificate meant that children of a certain age would be allowed to see the film if accompanied by an adult. 'X' certificate films were for adults only. Later, a more detailed system was felt to be necessary. Today, films considered suitable for all receive a 'U' certificate as before; 'borderline' films which are likely to be suitable for children but which should be vetted by their parents receive a 'PG' ('parental guidance') certificate. There are also '12', '15' and '18' certificates, which indicate the minimum ages required to see films with these certificates.

Outwitting the censor

Many directors have attempted to avoid the rules imposed by the British Board of Film Classification. This has often been in an attempt to include a potentially controversial but important scene in an **art film**. One famous example is the 1970 film made by the British director Ken Russell of D H Lawrence's novel *Women in Love*. At one point in the narrative, the two lead male characters, who may or may not be sexually attracted to each other, decide to explore their most primitive instincts by wrestling unclothed, 'cave-man' fashion. The censors at the time would not normally accept exposed male genitalia even in 'X' certificate films. Russell persuaded them of the importance of the scene, however, and said he would reduce the level of

The film director Ken Russell outwitted the censor in an ingenious way.

lighting to make the men's nudity less obvious. He then showed the scene to the censors again, whereupon the film was passed and granted a certificate (which allowed it to be released in cinemas). Russell later admitted that he in fact made no changes to the film at all! Presumably the censors had simply forgotten what the scene was like in the first place. Or might this mean that they were simply demonstrating their powers to the director? Did the film really require censorship at all?

25

Video and DVD

The availability of domestic recorded and recordable video media has added a new dimension to the process of censorship. At the same time, home video (the term will be used here to cover all the ways of recording and viewing moving images at home) is really an extension of earlier media, including film, television and 'home movies' – amateur films made on the home cine equipment that pre-dated the camcorder. This means that the home video medium has inherited much of the censorship debate from these earlier media, as well as creating new issues of its own.

A controversial horror video.

TRY THIS:
No warning?

The Video Standards Council adds short trailers to the beginning of videos. These explain the role of the organization, describe the types of BBFC certificates issued and indicate which certificate has been issued to the film being presented. If you can, see if these trailers are present on videos on which you would expect to find them. Ask an adult to check a few videos for you if you are not old enough to watch them yourself. Is this information present on every video? Is it missing from some videos where you feel such an explanation would have been useful? For instance, there are some confusing examples in the *Star Trek: Voyager* series. This is shown on TV during the early evening but when released on video some episodes have a 'PG' certificate (see page 24). Might this be explained on the videos? Is it?

The many faces of video

There are several ways in which video material is made available to and used by consumers. One is the rental or purchase of legitimate pre-recorded video material from libraries and high street outlets. This material is classified by a body called the Video Standards Council, which operates in a similar way to the **British Board of Film Classification** (**BBFC** – see page 24), and films released on video will generally inherit the **classification** they received for cinema release.

There are two types of pre-recorded videos which will not be granted a certificate and, ironically, they could not be more different. Certain videos are marked as 'exempt from classification'. These include certain types of documentary and instructional videos. If you check the packaging of, for example, a wildlife documentary, you may well find it marked with an 'E' – standing for 'exempt'. These informative videos are not thought to contain any potentially objectionable material. At the other extreme, certain types of illegal material will not be granted a certificate of any kind. In theory, this inhibits their **distribution**, as the material is effectively illegal, but of course it is relatively simple to bypass the system. For example, the videos can be duplicated in the outlets which sell them, or delivered privately. The police routinely raid premises selling this material and confiscate stock.

Video 'nasties'

In its early years, pre-recorded video was not subject to the same controls as film. Some opportunist film-makers realized that they could release material on video in the UK which would not be accepted by cinemas. The video 'nasty' was born. Video nasties featured extreme and **explicit** violence, with such titles as *Driller Killer, I Spit on Your Grave* and even *Killer Nun*. When **classification** was imposed upon videos in general, these video nasties largely disappeared from circulation in the UK. Recently, however, they have achieved **cult status** and some have been granted certificates, making them available once more. Interestingly, one of the reasons for their new-found acceptability has been the advance in **special effects** in mainstream cinema. People realized that these crudely-made, gory melodramas were in fact far too unrealistic to have a serious psychological effect on adult viewers.

This film was denied a video release for some years.

Computer software

The enormous variety of over-the-counter computer software that is now available has created yet another area in which censorship is needed, particularly in connection with PC and console games. Sensibly, much of this has drawn upon the type of **classification** used for film and video, with the required age noted on the packaging. Often this will conveniently coincide with the level of difficulty of the game, and many will also carry recommendations as to how old the player should be in order to be able to cope with the game successfully.

Software, games and morality

The ability of computer software to create complex fantasy worlds remains controversial. It has been claimed that, quite apart from turning people into terrible bores, many of the scenarios and characters in computer and console games are likely to encourage criminal activity and/or unrealistic ideas about female sexuality.

Might this never have happened had 'Grand Theft Auto' been banned?

One of the most extreme examples is 'Grand Theft Auto'. This game has, unsurprisingly, attracted enormous controversy. In the game scenario, you are a criminal in an American city. Your objective is to steal motor vehicles, using them to aid you in committing crimes of violence. Unsurprisingly, many objections have been raised by concerned adults. It has been suggested that the game glorifies street crime and that it will encourage such criminal behaviour in the real world. More subtly, in a **consumer society**, the very act of presenting an idea, however anti-social it may be, in a recognizable commercial package, can seem to be giving it 'official' approval.

Yet this example also indicates one of the most general points of censorship. The material itself is almost irrelevant – rather,

28

it is the reaction of those who avail themselves of the material that needs to be controlled. However, as this is impossible to do, the control must be applied to the material itself. If a player of 'Grand Theft Auto' is also involved in real-life car-jacking, is this because of the game? Or is it because they are the type of person who would commit these acts anyway? What of the many players who simply recognize the game for what it is and have no desire to commit acts of violence in real life? What do you think?

The knowing gamer

In fact, of course, the majority of people involved in the world of games software are intelligent, perceptive individuals with no more of a tendency towards criminal behaviour than anyone else. This often results in an element of irony in the way games are constructed, described and named. Games that involve wielding a weapon at enemies are known as 'shoot-'em-ups'. Adventure games frequently involve apparent acts of aggression, but these often have the slapstick quality of comic-strip violence. An example of this occurs in one of the famous 'Tomb Raider' games, in which the heroine, Lara Croft, tips her butler into a freezer! Another game is entitled 'Murder Death Kill' in an ironic reference to the non-gaming public's idea of computer games. One important aspect of this issue is the specialist nature of computer gaming, which inevitably leads to enthusiasts using a type of language among themselves that seems quite bizarre to outsiders. This is often evident in press reviews of computer games. One review of 'Sword of the Berserk: Gut's Rage' referred lovingly to the game as a 'slash-'em-up' and talked cheerfully of 'brutality' and slaughtering quotas. This review appeared in The Guardian – widely recognized as a high-quality newspaper. Is there a case here for further censorship? If not, why not?

The language used on this magazine cover seems to imply that its subject matter should perhaps be censored. But is this really the case?

29

The Internet

One consistent fact throughout the history of censorship has been that the guardians of public **morality** have always been several steps behind the advances made by communications technologists. This has meant that there has never been, and probably never will be, any form of censorship 'ready and waiting' for a new means of communication when it arises. Media such as home video and even simple devices such as the humble paper **duplicator** (a vital tool for reproducing **dissident** information in the **Soviet Union**, for example) have routinely taken the censors by surprise. That the Internet has come into being with very little in place by way of universally effective censorship is therefore hardly surprising.

Yet, unlike earlier media, its scope and potential for both good and ill is beyond measure. No wonder, then, that the control of the information available on the Internet is a key issue in the ongoing debate on censorship.

What might be censored?

Every type of information that might attract censorship, whether visual, textual, or even verbal, exists on the Internet. This includes material offering contentious political views, pornography, **corporate sabotage**, incitements to anti-social and criminal behaviour (such as instructions for making explosive devices), graphic

NOT A MEDIUM AT ALL?

It has been suggested that the Internet is not so much a medium as an environment. Media are channels for directed information, but the Internet is an enormous, constantly changing pool of data, which exists as the sum total of its users' knowledge and areas of interest. Users may 'dip into' this pool using web browser software, either choosing where to look or simply following their impulses, with results that can either be precise or wildly unpredictable. As with the real world, the Internet contains every imaginable type of information and opinion. It may well be that to censor the Internet effectively would be as hard or harder than trying to censor reality by removing every possibly contentious element from it.

ISP filtering software means that children can use the Internet without parents having to worry about what they will see.

depictions of extreme violence and so on. However, the Internet also offers enormous resources for education, the pursuit of hobbies and interests, valuable professional information, on-line shopping and a great deal of harmless fun and fascination for adults and children alike.

Freedom

There are also issues of personal liberty. For example, in the real world, there are no laws against holding extreme views, sharing these views with others or even acting upon them provided these actions remain within the law. Should there be different sets of laws for the Internet? What do you think? One counter-argument is that certain forms of freedom can only exist by repressing the freedom of others. The white supremacist movement in the USA is one example of this. There are also some very subtle forms of censorship used by such organizations as BBC Online, where messages will sometimes be rejected from bulletin boards for undisclosed reasons.

Where does responsibility lie?

Censorship of the Internet does exist, but unlike most other forms of censorship it is largely motivated by commercial interest and corporate public relations. Responsibility for large-scale censorship has so far mainly fallen on **Internet service providers (ISPs)**. It is in the interest of these companies to ensure that as many people as possible use their services. Many of their users will be children, or parents, or adults who do not wish to come across offensive material, or companies who do not want their employees accessing such material. For this reason, many ISP's provide **filtering**

software that can prevent the material being accessed. Of course, the most important controllers of Internet content are responsible members of the public.

David Duke, an American white supremacist.

CASE STUDY

David Duke is an American white supremacist. He believes that black people are inferior to white people and uses a website to promote his ideas. He does not use the site to suggest any form of illegal action. Should he be entitled to express these ideas freely on the Internet? Or does his freedom to do so erode the freedom of others – in this case, black people – by prejudicing others against them?

Art

Even in democratic societies, art has always had a strange relationship with censorship. This is partly outlined on pages 24–25, which deal with how this relationship came to influence the censorship of the theatre and films. Generally, artistic expression has enjoyed a level of freedom that has not always been available to other forms of communication. There are many reasons for this. One is the philosophical aspect of art – it is considered to be the product of sophisticated thinking and therefore its content, whatever it may be, is there for a good reason. Another reason is the

background of those people who, in European culture at least, are assumed to be interested in art. They are expected to be intelligent, educated and upper- or upper-middle-class. This is taken to mean that if they are exposed to art which includes, say, nudity or horrific imagery, they will understand the artistic intention and not react to it at a directly sexual or 'copy-cat' level. How likely do you think this is to be true?

Expression and repression

In other societies, however, art has been subject to very direct forms of censorship. In the days of the **Soviet Union**, for example, all art which did not express images acceptable to the ruling Communist Party was heavily suppressed. Many of the traditional subjects of art were against Party ideology. Religion has inspired many of the most widely admired paintings and sculptures for many centuries. However, the Communist regime discouraged religious worship, which placed faith ahead of duty to the state. Artworks that depicted other forms of government, such as portraits of royalty and nobility, were also inappropriate (the rule of the Communist Party in the Soviet Union had replaced an imperial regime), as was art that implied middle-class, materialistic values. This left relatively little that was, in fact, acceptable. The result was that much Soviet art of the period was dominated by supposedly 'realistic' depictions of workers labouring in industry or agriculture, looking vigorous and happy. Much of this art appeared in the form of posters, which could be seen easily by the general population.

Censorship in the Soviet Union resulted in 'ideologically correct' art such as this.

The reality, of course, was rather different, in that manual labour under the Soviet regime was no different from manual labour anywhere else – it still got you and your clothes dirty and left you tired and hungry at the end of the day. This was in effect a double dose of information control. Not only was original art subject to censorship, but the content of the supposedly realistic art that replaced it was also heavily controlled.

A recurring image

As art is, by definition, highly visible, it is perhaps an obvious target for censorship. It is therefore something of a **paradox** that this realistic Soviet art has itself become a symbol of oppressive censorship and has been used by other artists and writers to convey this. In his novel *A Clockwork Orange* (1962), the British author Anthony Burgess describes an imaginary future society which may or may not have become controlled by the

Of course, the reality was the same in the Soviet Union as anywhere else.

Soviet regime, or something very like it – the teenagers of the day speak a Russian-influenced dialect, for example. The main character, a violent teenager named Alex, lives in a block of flats which has a large mural in the lobby called 'The Dignity of Labour'. It features a group of workers going about their tasks in a style that is clearly meant to invite comparison with Soviet art. It is worth adding here that the book itself appeared in two versions. One ended with the implication that Alex would mend his ways and become a responsible citizen, whereas the other did not. This is said to have happened as a result of different publishers in different territories having different ideas about how their readers would want the book to end. Is this a form of censorship? If not, what is it? What do you think?

33

Music

It is perhaps to be expected that music that involves any form of text, from folk song to pop song to opera, can be subject to censorship, as the words can convey information in a highly memorable way. Some examples are the old English political song 'Lilliburlero' and protest folk songs from the second half of this century, such as 'If I Had a Hammer'. However, why should instrumental music, which in itself can carry no **explicit** message, also have attracted some of the most aggressive censorship in history?

Music and context

In fact, music does not and cannot exist in a vacuum. The composer, the performers, the audience, the circumstances under which the music is heard and any recording or broadcasting organizations which may also be involved are all important elements. What is perhaps most important is the composer's background and motivation. The music he or she creates can be seen as representing a viewpoint that may conflict with that of society as a whole, or, more specifically, those who wish to control society. There are many examples in recent history.

Degenerate music

The **Nazi** Party rose to political power in Germany in the 1930s. Central to the Nazi philosophy was the belief that the indigenous inhabitants of Germany (an ethnic group which the Nazis referred to as 'Aryans') were innately superior to other races.

The music of Berthold Goldschmidt was suppressed by the Nazis.

ETHNICITY AND MUSIC

It would be nice to think that ideas about the innate superiority of one ethnic group over another are finally being dismissed. However, **disinformation** about, for example, the musical abilities of various races persists today. The black American composer Anthony Braxton, for example, has written a whole cycle of large-scale operas and holds a university professorship, but he is known primarily as a jazz musician and is rarely accepted in other areas of music.

This notion of racial superiority is probably as old as humanity itself and it survives today in various forms, some very subtle, some overt and extreme (like the beliefs held by politically active white supremacists – see page 31).

The Nazis believed that certain ethnic groups, such as Jews, were particularly inferior. This eventually led to the mass extermination known as the Holocaust, but there were also many instances of cultural **oppression**. The work of many Jewish composers such as Goldschmidt and Korngold was condemned by the Nazis as degenerate. This meant that their music was somehow uncivilized and not fit to be heard. As a result of this the music was banned and the composers themselves were persecuted, with many of them having to escape abroad. In reality, of course, the music itself was irrelevant; rather, the Nazis simply wished to erase all traces of Jewish culture. In the event, several Jewish composers, including Korngold, fled to America, where they became very successful in composing for both the concert hall and the cinema. Their music is now widely recorded and performed, but it has still taken half a century for the censorship imposed by the Nazis to be fully overcome.

South Africa

During the **apartheid** era in South Africa, the country's national broadcasting organization set up special services supposedly to record and broadcast indigenous music. This gave the impression that black South African music and culture was being carefully preserved by the country's white rulers. In reality, the music was heavily censored. Any songs which related in any way to freedom or struggle were excluded, as was any music which might have reinforced the desire for black independence. Archived recordings which might have had a similar effect were sometimes damaged to prevent them being broadcast. Often black musicians would be invited into recording studios, supposedly to add to the government's collection of traditional black music. In fact, the musicians were discouraged from recording any music which implied discontent or unhappiness. Instead, they were expected to promote a positive image of life under apartheid. This was a particularly destructive form of censorship, as the musicians involved usually had very little money and the opportunity to do some well-paid recording sessions was hard to ignore. Many black South African musicians whose music appealed to audiences abroad chose to emigrate in order to avoid the regime's censorship and oppression.

'★★★★★, ★★★★ my ★★★★!'

A less important but rather better-publicized process has been, and continues to be, the censorship of lyrics that include **expletives** in both rock and hip-hop. This rarely involves outright banning, but is more likely to involve the prohibition of radio play unless an alternative version is recorded (see pages 20–21). This is a strategy that has been adopted by many bands and their record companies over the years. The Rolling Stones, the Stranglers and The Beautiful South have all opted to hear their music on the radio in a cleaned-up form rather than not at all. The original versions are still available in the shops, but the wide adoption of stickers on such discs advising parents that the songs contain explicit lyrics has seemed to offer a workable compromise.

Theatre

Whether or not a theatrical performance is likely to be subject to censorship depends on many largely unrelated factors. These include the political climate in the country in which the performance is taking place, current views on such subjects as nudity and, most importantly, where the idea of 'theatre' begins and ends.

Art versus entertainment

In the loosest sense, a theatrical performance could be taken to include any occasion where an audience watches some kind of event or series of events involving one or more real people. This means that a performance of Shakespeare's *Macbeth* and a live show involving **unsimulated** sexual intercourse (illegal in the UK) have more in common than might occur to anyone involved in either. In this context, less **explicit** shows involving strippers of either sex are perhaps a borderline case. Indeed, such events can easily take place in a theatre that would also host a performance of *Macbeth*. In this situation, the process of censorship is partly a matter of the theatre management's judgement as to whether such an event is acceptable. After that, the standard legal restrictions apply, simply meaning that those under the age of 18 will not be admitted.

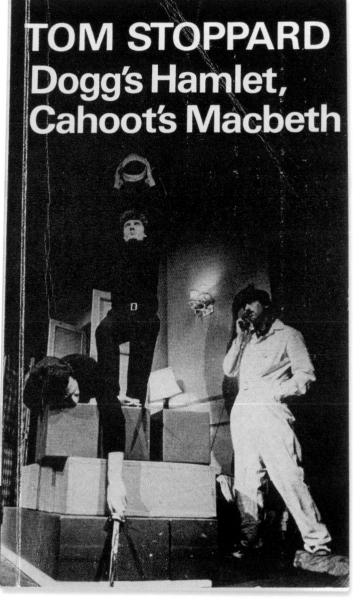

Theatrical censorship is one of the themes in this humorous play.

36

The theatre and political repression

Far more important, however, is the fact that conventional art theatre has always been a powerful political weapon. During its early history, it could be used to manipulate information in all manner of ways. Shakespeare's history play *Henry V* is a good example of this. During the play, we learn how the young English king is legally entitled to claim rulership of France. This he does, despite encountering some resistance, and, after a charmingly fumbling attempt to learn French, he persuades the French princess Katherine to marry him and they all live happily ever after. In reality, Henry led an invading army into France on the highly questionable basis of an obscure and archaic European law governing inheritance. He slaughtered large numbers of French people and then ensured that the reigning families of the two warring countries were bound together by marriage. The saying that history is always written by the winning side appears to be entirely true – and it is generally censored in favour of the winning side in the process.

An **oppressive** political regime will routinely attempt to censor and suppress any form of theatre that does not support it. One notable example is the case of the Czech dramatist Pavel Kohout. During the 1970s, after the **Soviet Union** had taken direct control of Czechoslovakia (now the Czech Federation), many people were forced into other jobs. They were those who worked in professions that could be used to spread **dissident** thinking, such as writing and the theatre. This was an extremely oppressive form of censorship as it simply prevented many theatrical productions from happening at all. Kohout and an actor named Pavel Landovksy found a way around this by starting a small, highly mobile theatre group which performed by invitation in private flats in Prague, the Czech capital. This was an ingenious way of opposing the regime's attempts to censor the theatrical profession. Not only would it have proved difficult to keep track of the group's activities, but there would be no way of proving that the events really amounted to theatrical performances. The British playwright Tom Stoppard, a friend of Kohout, preserved these events in his satirical play *Dogg's Hamlet, Cahoot's Macbeth*.

CASE STUDY

Occasionally an exaggerated sense of **propriety** can result in some rather eccentric attempts at censorship. The theatre provides some good examples. Alan Bennett is another British playwright who has written a very funny play with a Czech connection. In it the celebrated Czech author Franz Kafka, his parents and his agent, Max Brod, somehow all turn up at an insurance agent's flat in Leeds (the play is big on surreal humour). Bennett called the play *Kafka's Dick*. One provincial theatre took exception to the title and advertised it as *Kafka's Duck*.

Censorship and politics

While censorship is of course a direct concern of the media and of the individuals who obtain their information from the media (that is, all of us), it is also important to consider why censorship exists at all. The political arena is one of the most significant areas in which censorship and other forms of information control are put to use, and never more so than during time of war.

Government censorship

The First World War provides a good example of how censorship in the UK operated at the highest level of information, while at the same time filtering down to the general population in an attempt to ensure 'grass roots' support for government policy. In 1909 tension between the UK and Germany was growing. In this atmosphere of general **paranoia** (German spies were believed to be everywhere), the government formed a new Directorate of Military Intelligence. This led, in the following year, to the passing of the second Official Secrets Act (an earlier, relatively restrained, version already existed). This act gave the government of the day extraordinary powers of censorship. It hinged on the notion of what information was or was not held to be 'in the public interest'.

In practice, the Act not only empowered the government to withhold information from the press and the general public, but it also allowed information to be withheld from Parliament, which supposedly represented the interests of the people.

The Press Bureau

At the beginning of the War, in 1914, the government set up an organization called the Press Bureau. This consisted of four censors, twenty-one assistant censors and six other assistants. They were organized into departments which received telegrams, press information and other potentially sensitive material. The departments then issued them in a censored form, removing anything that

This wartime letter containing sensitive information was not delivered to its intended recipient.

might give hints into military secrets or other information that might hinder the war effort. An official memo issued to the Bureau's censors detailed their duties as follows:

- 'to prevent the publication of news injurious to the naval and military operations of the British Empire;
- to prevent the publication of news likely to cause needless alarm and distress among the civil population;
- to prevent the publication of news objectionable on political grounds: news, for example, calculated to injure the susceptibilities of other Allies.'

Prior to this, the Home Secretary had informed Parliament that the public had 'a reasonable right to expect that no news will be published in the press except such news as is furnished in the Bureau'. This was a rather alarming statement which the Prime Minister later qualified by saying that in fact 'all information which can be given without prejudice to the public interest shall be given fully and at once'. Conveniently, this second statement sounded like a partial retraction of the sweeping measures proposed in the first. However, as the public could not know whether or not they were receiving

Wartime briefings such as this one would have resulted in a great deal of censored information.

their information 'fully and at once', the government had ensured that its powers of censorship were, in fact, undiminished.

FROM THE GREATEST TO THE LEAST

The Press Bureau was subsequently disbanded, but this historical example shows that, even in democratic countries, governments are always prepared to adopt severe measures for censoring information should the need arise. Is this happening now? What kind of information might be being withheld from the British population today?

During the First World War, the newspapers broadly accepted the principle of censorship. However, even more personal communications, such as letters sent by members of the forces to their families back home, could be intercepted and censored during wartime. One reason for this was to avoid the possibility of sensitive information falling into the hands of enemy spies. Unfortunately, this meant that many letters were returned to their senders.

Censorship and society

If we look at the history of censorship, as well as current ideas about the process in different cultures across the world, it becomes clear that there have always been and still are enormous differences in what should or should not be considered for censorship and why. Furthermore, the authority to censor information can rest with different individuals or groups across different cultures. Within any culture, views as to what should or should not be permitted will vary enormously from one individual to the next.

Whose views?

You can easily identify differing attitudes to censorship among the people you know. A young parent may feel that sex and violence should be eliminated from television programmes likely to be seen by children, but may have no objection to these elements featuring in a programme for adults broadcast late in the evening. An older person who grew up with a more conservative attitude to sexuality may object to sex being depicted on television at all. The same older person may also have grown up before racism became recognized as a serious issue and see no problem with racist jokes, unless they themselves belong to an ethnic group which has been the victim of this kind of demeaning 'humour'. Younger people who have grown up in a more integrated society may well find this kind of material highly objectionable. Different people may apply differing sets of moral standards to an issue but seek the same outcome. For example, some people would like to see

all forms of **erotic** imagery involving women banned simply because they find public sexual displays to be rude and objectionable. Other people would like to see them banned because they believe that these images are degrading and insulting to women.

CASE STUDY

Differing religious beliefs can have an enormous effect on the types of material individuals believe should be censored. One of the best-known recent examples was the case of Salman Rushdie's novel *The Satanic Verses*. This book caused anger among certain sections of the Muslim community (even resulting in a death threat being made against the author) because it insulted their religious beliefs. One interesting aspect of this episode was the way in which it drew attention to the UK's **blasphemy** laws, effectively a form of censorship that could restrict material that insulted the Christian religion. Some Muslims proposed, not unreasonably, that these laws should be extended to cover all religions practised in the UK, of which Islam was one.

No censorship?

Some individuals and organizations advocate the complete removal of all forms of censorship, pointing to examples such as the less stringent laws governing **hard pornography** in the USA. The arguments are firstly, that the censorship of material simply drives it **underground** without impeding those who wish to obtain it. They will simply do so by illegal means. Secondly, it is claimed that

making every type of information and visual image readily available will simply defuse the whole issue. What would you say?

These arguments in fact carry with them the idea that censorship is a form of artificial regulation that is somehow imposed on society. Yet the control of information seems to be built into the way we think. As soon as you decide not to call someone a rude name, or choose not to give someone a detailed description of the injuries arising from a traffic accident you witnessed, or choose not to tell your younger brother or sister an unpleasantly scary bedtime story, you are censoring information that you have and that you could pass on if you chose to do so. This decision-making process is voluntary and conscious. Is censorship in general nothing more than a larger version of this process? What do you think?

Salman Rushdie received a death threat from angry Muslims when his novel *The Satanic Verses* was published.

CASE STUDY

When racism first became recognized as a serious social issue in the UK there were many well-intentioned moves to eliminate racist ideas from British culture. One example of this is the children's story book Little Black Sambo by Helen Bannerman, which some public libraries removed from their shelves – a very obvious example of censorship – because the word 'sambo' had become a derogatory term for black people. The book had in fact been written in 1899 and was a very old-fashioned fairy tale about an African boy. Was this a good idea? Read the book and see what you think.

41

Censorship
and the future

Censorship is a very sensitive subject and most educated people have views about it. You can prove this by simply conducting an informal survey. Try making a list based on the examples given throughout this book and quiz your friends, family and teachers as to whether they think censorship should be applied in each case, and if so, to what extent. You will probably find a wide range of opinion, but what is most interesting is that most people will at least have an opinion. You are likely to get lots of 'yes' or 'no' answers, but very few 'don't knows', even when the situation being described is not one which is personally familiar to your **informant**.

This is because censorship is strongly linked in people's minds to questions of **ethics** and **morality**. People are taught what is held to be good and bad from the time they are babies (eating your food properly is 'good', throwing it on the floor is 'bad'). The subject of censorship, however, is a no-win situation. Allowing people to be exposed to information which they find offensive or frightening may be bad, but surely withholding information from people is a form of deception, which is equally bad?

Is no answer the best answer?

The balance between these two factors, both now and in the future, is at the heart of the ongoing debate on censorship. Perhaps the ideal solution is that the dilemma is never resolved at all. Might this ensure that the arguments on both sides are constantly being put forward, so that there is no chance of either viewpoint disappearing from society altogether? What do you think?

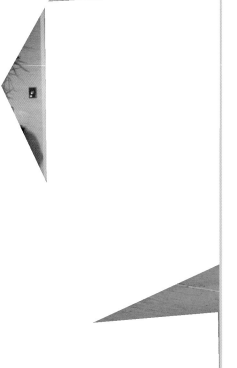

In *Fahrenheit 451*, books are illegal and are burned whenever they are discovered. Don't try this at home.

Things to come?

Many authors have been fascinated by the implications of censorship, and there are many novels and films with imaginative stories showing how censorship could operate if taken to extremes – that is, if the anti-censorship **lobby** was effectively silenced.

In Ray Bradbury's novel *Fahrenheit 451*, a future is imagined in which the printed word has been banned altogether. This is enforced by 'firemen', whose job is not to save people and property from fires but to seek out hidden books and burn them. Books are illegal and regarded as evil because, as one of the characters explains, they encourage people to form their own ideas instead of just participating in whatever the majority are doing. Of course, a society in which everyone has the same set of ideas about everything is the easiest kind of society to control. If you think about the ways in which this might apply to you and to the people you know, you may be unpleasantly surprised at just how often everyone appears to have the same views, do the same things and live pretty similar lives.

George Orwell's *1984* is a biting attack upon all forms of dictatorship. In the novel, the UK has become part of a vast super-state ('Oceania') in which all forms of information are totally controlled by the government (called 'the Party'). Records are routinely falsified in order to deceive the population. Every room has a 'telescreen', which both issues orders and monitors people's private lives for any trace of **dissident** behaviour. The main character, Winston Smith, works for the Ministry of Truth, a government department which is responsible for producing propaganda and for changing the information contained in books, newspapers and so on, so that it supports the Party's version of history. This book has been filmed several times.

In *1984*, the dictatorial government is depicted in the form of a single authority figure, 'Big Brother'.

Finally...

...and just for fun, have a look back through this book to see if there's any information which you think has been presented by the author in such a way as to try to influence your own views!

Glossary

anthropomorphic in the shape of a human being

apartheid segregation or discrimination of people based on ethnic background

art film film that is intended as a work of art rather than popular entertainment

arthouse a type of cinema that shows art films

blasphemy statements that are disrespectful or violently contrary to established religious beliefs

British Board of Film Classification (BBFC) organization that checks the content of films and decides what kind of audience should be allowed to see each film

classification process of grouping things together according to the similarities they have

colloquial describes informal speech usually used by people who know each other well

consumer society society that depends on people buying goods and services

corporate sabotage secretly interfering with the activities of a commercial organization

cult status status achieved when a work of art, literature or music and/or its creator attracts a relatively small but well-informed and dedicated following

disinformation detailed but completely inaccurate or untrue information

dissident describes a person who disagrees strongly with the actions of their government

distribution process whereby products are sold and delivered to shops

duplicator hand-operated machine that can copy printed paper using chemicals, requiring no electricity

erotic tastefully sexy

ethics concept of right and wrong

expletive swear word or obscenity

explicit detailed and accurate, or leaving nothing to the imagination

freedom of speech freedom to express any view without fear of punishment

free press newspapers and magazines not being subject to government control

hard pornography explicit pornography that depicts detailed and obviously genuine sexual activity

heresy statement that refutes conventional religious views

informant someone who answers questions during research

Inquisition a tribunal set up to investigate claims of heresy

intellectual freedom freedom to hold or consider any opinion or theory

Internet service provider (ISP) company which provides connections to the Internet

IRA the Irish Republican Army

left-wing political principles theories

based on socialism, the idea that goods should be distributed equally

lobby group of people who share an opinion and present it to those in authority

media barons powerful business people who may own a variety of media, for example both publishing and broadcasting companies

media landscape term coined by the American philosopher Marshall McLuhan to describe the world of information created by the media

minor person who is legally recognized as being too young to take decisions on certain issues

morality concept of good and bad

moral philosophy formal study of ideas arising from morality

Nazi member of the National Socialist Party in Germany; led by Adolf Hitler

oppression aggressive, continued process of control

paradox situation that appears to contradict itself

paranoia the unjustified belief that a person or group is being persecuted

platform opportunity to convey an opinion to a group of people

propriety accepted standards of politeness

revue theatrical performance that mixes songs and short dramatic items

samizdat Russian word meaning 'self-publication', used to describe controversial writings circulated in typed or copied form during the Soviet regime

satire literature or drama that humorously attacks important people and/or their views

Sinn Fein section of the IRA devoted to political rather than para-military action

slot particular time in a broadcasting schedule

Soviet Union group of countries formerly controlled by Russia

special effects ways of simulating fantastic or dangerous events for film, video and television

tableaux vivants static theatrical displays

taboo forbidden idea or action that is deeply embedded in a culture

talk radio radio programming that involves speech but not music

transsexual person who chooses to have their gender changed through surgery

underground alternative culture or political action

unsimulated not faked

watershed when used in connection with broadcasting, the time after which adult material may be transmitted

Contacts

ADVERTISING STANDARDS AUTHORITY

2 Torrington Place
London WC1E 7HW
020 7580 5555

ARTICLE 19: THE INTERNATIONAL CENTRE AGAINST CENSORSHIP

Lancaster House, 33 Islington High Street
London N1 9H
020 7278 9292

International human rights organization which campaigns for the right to freedom of expression and information and which defends victims of censorship.

BRITISH BOARD OF FILM CLASSIFICATION

3 Soho Square
London W1V 6HD
020 7439 7961

BROADCASTING STANDARDS COMMISSION

7 The Sanctuary
London SW1P 3JS
020 7233 0544

Deals with issues relating to violence, sexual conduct and matters of taste and decency in broadcasting.

CAMPAIGN FOR FREEDOM OF INFORMATION

Suite 102, 16 Baldwins Gardens
London EC1N 7RJ
020 7831 7477
www.cfoi.org.uk

Campaigns for public access to official records, amendments to the Official Secrets Act and seeks to compel private companies to reveal undisclosed information which is in the public interest.

CAMPAIGN FOR PRESS AND BROADCASTING FREEDOM

6 Cynthia Street
London N1 9JF
020 7278 4430
www.cpbf.demon.co.uk
Campaigns for democracy and accountability in the media.

PRESS COMPLAINTS COMMISSION

1 Salisbury Square
London EC4 8AE
020 7353 1284

In Australia

OFFICE OF FILM & LITERATURE CLASSIFICATION

Locked Bag 3
Haymarket
NSW 1240
(02) 9289 7100
Email: oflcswitch@oflc.gov.au
www.oflc.gov.au

THE AUSTRALIAN BROADCASTING AUTHORITY (ABA)

PO Box Q500,
Queen Victoria Building NSW 1230
Australia
+61 2 9334 7700
Free call (Australia only): *1 800 22 6667*
www.aba.gov.au
An independent federal statutory authority responsible for the regulation of free-to-air radio and television, pay TV, digital broadcasting and Internet content in Australia.

**ELECTRONIC FRONTIERS
AUSTRALIA INC.**
PO Box 382
North Adelaide SA 5006
Australia.
07 3424 0201
Email: mail@efa.org.au
www.efa.org.au
A non-profit national organization formed to protect and promote the civil liberties of users and operators of computer based communications systems.

Further reading

Most of these books are written for adults, so you may need help in finding the information you need.

Index on Censorship
Writers and Scholars International
www. indexoncensorship.org
Published every two months, this journal in the form of a paperback book carries essays about how information is being controlled today, with a strong emphasis on human rights.

The Republic
Plato
Penguin Books
One of the earliest pro-censorship books. You may need help to find the relevant part!

Ways of Seeing
John Berger
Penguin Books
A famous book about how information is presented – and controlled – in art. It deals with sophisticated ideas but is fairly easy to read.

Media Focus: Advertising
Roger Thomas
Heinemann Library
This book contains some examples of how advertisers such as Coca-Cola attempt to control the environment in which their advertisements appear.

Media Focus: Magazines and comics
Roger Thomas
Heinemann Library
This book includes a short section about how censorship can affect the media.

Burning Issues
rene.efa.org.au
This website provides a good overview of censorship in Australia. The site itself is anti-censorship, but it also provides good historical information.

Index

Titles in the *What's at issue* series include:

Hardback   0 431 03559 8

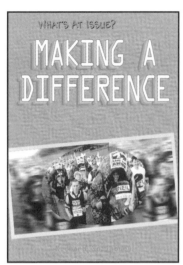

Hardback   0 431 03555 5

Hardback   0 431 03554 7

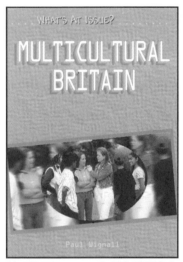

Hardback   0 431 03560 1

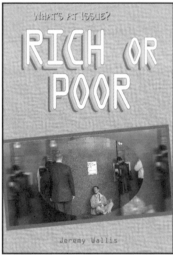

Hardback   0 431 03556 3

Hardback   0 431 03557 1

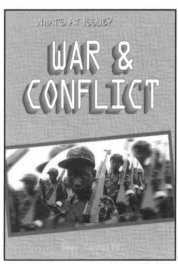

Hardback   0 431 03558 X

Find out about the other titles in this series on our website www.heinemann.co.uk/library